Friends 4 Ever

For one groovy gal, aka editor Suzanne Nelson

— J.H.

For my marvelous Maria!

— T.M.

ISBN 0-439-86647-2

12 11 10 9 8 7 6 5 4 3 2 1   6 7 8 9 10 11/0

Printed in the U.S.A.
First printing, September 2006
Book design by Carla Siegel

Friends 4 Ever

For Girls Only

A Guide to Great Girl-Bonding Activities

by Jo Hurley
Illustrated by Taia Morley

Scholastic Inc.
New York   Toronto   London   Auckland   Sydney
Mexico City   New Delhi   Hong Kong   Buenos Aires

Rachel

Name: Rachel

Nickname: Red

Style: Artsy

Hobbies: Crafts, music, acting

Favorite Place: Theater (onstage!)

Favorite Sport: Swimming

Favorite Snack: Granola and yogurt

Hidden Talent: Always optimistic

Sometimes Known As: Drama Queen

Sam

Name: Samantha

Nickname: Sam

Style: Casual

Hobbies: Hiking, biking

Favorite Place: The gym

Favorite Sport: Soccer, skiing, sailing

Favorite Snack: Energy bar

Hidden Talent: Making people laugh

Sometimes Known As: The Athlete

JESSIE

Name: Jessica

Nickname: Jessie

Style: Girly

Hobbies: Reading, writing, babysitting

Favorite Place: The library

Favorite Sport: Tennis

Favorite Snack: Corn chips

Hidden Talent: Great Listener

Sometimes Known As: The Great Brain

Name: Elizabeth

Nickname: Libby

Style: Glam

Hobbies: Volunteering, cooking

Favorite Place: Anywhere with lots of people

Favorite Sport: Dance

Favorite Snack: Fruit salad

Hidden Talent: Never at a loss for words

Sometimes Known As: Party Girl

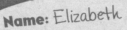

Libby

We Stick Together Like Superglue

Best friends stay close by giving lots of HUGS.

Squeeeeeeze!

We stay in touch in person . . .
and on the phone . . .
wherever we go . . .
whatever we do. . . .

The thing about best friends is that we know all about one another—even the secret stuff.

In good times and bad, we're totally bonded. That's why they call us **Friends 4-Ever!**

Let's Get This Party Started!

The best way to get a team of friends together is to plan a small, medium, or megaPARTY. Ever since Libby, Jessie, Rachel, and I were little, we've had the best times together planning parties of all kinds. Here's the thing: Parties never fail to a) cheer us up, b) bring us closer together, and c) make us laugh. And that last part is sooooo important. Because no one makes you laugh like a best friend!

"Get This Party Started" Checklist

Every party planner needs a checklist of things to do. Make your own list on a colorful piece of paper and put it on the fridge where you'll see it all the time!

Getting Started

★ Decide on the date, place, and style of the party. (In the following pages, we have included tons of cool ideas for you.)

★ Make up the guest list. Think carefully about who you'll invite— and who you won't. Try not to hurt anyone's feelings by leaving them off the list.

★ Plan the menu. (Check out some of the cool recipes on pages 22–26.)

- ★ For formal parties, mail invitations. For casual parties, e-mail invitations or call your guests to invite them.

- ★ Decide what table settings, decorations, centerpieces, and music you'll use. Pick things that everyone will enjoy.

Before the Party

- ★ Clean up your room and get the rest of your space in order. You don't want party guests tripping over laundry or your little brother's blocks.

- ★ Work with your mom or dad on a shopping list. Stock up on snacks and drinks. Sometimes parties are more about munching than major meals.

- ★ Make decorations early so you won't be doing it at the last minute!

- ★ Prepare party items beforehand, like desserts or goody bags. Everyone loves a surprise treat.

- ★ Unearth your secret stash of fashion magazines, CDs, board games, or photo albums that your guests might like to use.

- ★ Make sure you have film for your camera (if it's 35 mm), or that you have space on your memory card (if it's digital). And don't forget to charge your batteries.

- ★ Rent DVDs or video games, depending on your party theme.

Party Time

- ★ Put on mood music, wear your coolest outfit, and have an AWESOME time!

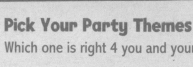

Pick Your Party Themes
Which one is right 4 you and your 4-Ever Friends?

Pop Music

★ Dress like you're auditioning for American Idol—or like your favorite pop star.

★ Rent a karaoke machine or get one of those cool portable microphones for a lip-synching contest.

★ Borrow Mom and Dad's video camera and make your own party music video.

Haunted House

★ Dress like your favorite monster.

★ Rent spooky/funny flicks like *Abbott and Costello Meet Frankenstein* or the original *Godzilla*.

★ Play board games, like Clue, together, or read ghost stories to your friends by flashlight.

Sporty

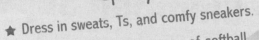

- ★ Dress in sweats, Ts, and comfy sneakers.
- ★ Go bowling or play a game of softball in your backyard.

- ★ Schedule the party during the play-offs of your favorite sport.

Movie Star

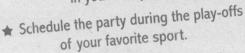

- ★ Dress up for maximum glamour.
- ★ Buy copies of all the latest glossy Hollywood gossip magazines.
- ★ Give everyone a goody bag with lip gloss and cool plastic shades (like the bags they give the real stars at awards shows).

Retro–Disco

- ★ Dress in tie-dye, platform shoes, and glitter.
- ★ Have a dance-off with tunes from the seventies and eighties.
- ★ Serve Disco Fries, aka french fries with melted cheese and gravy on top.

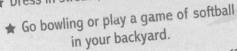

Super Slumber Super

Who to Invite: Your best buds! Four to six friends is a good number.

What to Expect: Lots of time together talking, playing, munching, and swapping secrets—and dares. Be prepared for anything!

When to Have It: Usually a Friday or Saturday night—but not a school night. Of course, anytime goes in the summer!

What to Remember: Sometimes sleeping away from home can be hard—even if you're with your best buds. Be sensitive if a friend is feeling homesick or awkward for any reason.

One summer, Sam and I planned an outdoor slumber party for the four of us—and it was *too* cool. It was an under-the-stars campout in my brother's old tent. We squished together in sleeping bags, pulled out our flashlights, and told ghost stories. We couldn't stop laughing!

Five MUST-BRING Things for Your Slumber Party:

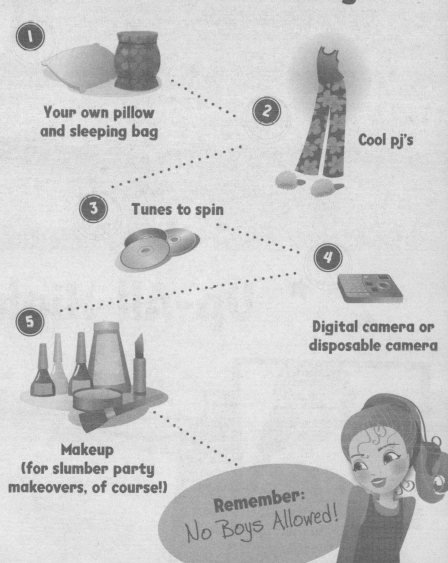

1 Your own pillow and sleeping bag

2 Cool pj's

3 Tunes to spin

4 Digital camera or disposable camera

5 Makeup (for slumber party makeovers, of course!)

Remember: No Boys Allowed!

Slumber Party Activities

 ★ Decorate pillowcases with fabric markers and puffy paints.

★ Turn your living room into a runway and have a pajama fashion show.

★ Plan a late-night scavenger hunt (into the kitchen for a snack!).

★ Play Twister, Trivia, or other board games.

★ Have pillow fights. (May the fluffiest pillow win!)

★ Tell jokes and riddles (take a good book out of the library that you can share).

Up-All-Night

Definitely don't play pranks at your slumber party. You need to be supercareful so that no one's feelings get hurt. Once at a huge sleepover, these girls I didn't even really like filled my hair with hairspray and gunk and let it dry in this totally weird way. Everyone laughed but it wasn't fun. Not at all!

Conversation Ideas

Let's make up lyrics to our own songs!

Tell me what I'm supposed to wear to the school dance!

Make Your Own Mystery Party

Mystery parties take a lot of planning and your guests should really want to play roles and participate. First, the party host writes a mini-mystery. Each guest is assigned to play a role, one of the characters in the mystery. The criminal must not give away her identity.

Guests come to the party dressed as characters. The more guests at the party, the better! After guests arrive, they should mingle. As they do this, a "crime" takes place. Characters begin to gossip, drop hints, and eavesdrop on one another. Clues are revealed.

All guests must try to figure out who is the criminal. When she has been correctly identified and proven guilty, she must admit her crime.

Mystery Theme Ideas

COUNTRY-WESTERN

Call it: Hoedown Horror

Costume: Red bandanna, cowboy boots, horseshoe T-shirt

PIRATE
Call it: Danger on the High Seas
Costume: Eye patch, sword, vest over white shirt

ENGLISH VICTORIAN
Call it: Murder at the Manor
Costume: Dress with petticoat, long gloves, veil

CIRCUS CARNIVAL
Call it: Big Flop Under the Big Top
Costume: Clown nose, big shoes, ballerina tutu with polka-dot tights

HELLO
my name is

DON'T FORGET! GET NAME TAGS FOR THE PARTY. EACH GUEST MUST WRITE HER CHARACTER NAME ON HER TAG SO SHE CAN BE IDENTIFIED.

Invitation Ideas:

★ Cut up invitations into pieces like a puzzle!

★ Write information backward so it must be held up to a mirror to be read!

YOU'RE INVITED!

★ Write in secret code!

25 . 15 . 21   ' 23 . 5   9 . 13 . 24 . 9 . 20 . 5 . 4 !

18

How to Write Your Own Mystery Party
by Rachel (aka Drama Queen)

I asked my English teacher to help me write my own mystery—and she gave me some great ideas.

1. Start with the end. Always know your crime before you start writing the rest of the mystery.

2. Look in the newspaper for true crime and mystery ideas. Some of the best mystery ideas come from real life. Or grab a book of mini-mysteries like Encyclopedia Brown from the library for inspiration.

3. Your main character is the person who keeps the plot moving. Give him or her a lot to do. Make up a strong cast of minor characters, too.

4. Identify the fact that your main character has a problem.

5. Make a list of clues and red herrings (clues that don't lead anywhere or that lead to the wrong person).

6. Use setting to your advantage. Set your mystery in the fog, the dark, a deserted castle, or all of the above. Whatever you do— make it ultramysterious!

Inside Your Mystery...

Why Not Try Some of These Props?

- ★ Fake telephone
- ★ Briefcase
- ★ Camera
- ★ Black cape
- ★ Cane
- ★ Fake money
- ★ Fake jewels
- ★ Musical instrument
- ★ False beard or mustache

Mystery Goody Bag Goods

- ★ Mini-magnifiers
- ★ Mystery books
- ★ Bookmark
- ★ Puzzles
- ★ Flashlights
- ★ Notepads

Cook Up a YUMMY Party!

Let your tummy do all the talking at your next get-together. Getting good friends into the kitchen to make some food is a great way to work together—and really dish at the same time.

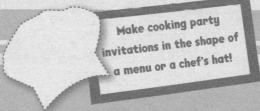

Make cooking party invitations in the shape of a menu or a chef's hat!

Libby's Kitchen Safety Tips

★ Make sure your cooking is being supervised by an adult!

★ Watch out for steam when cooking, because it can cause serious burns.

★ Be careful where you put knives. You don't want anyone to get hurt.

★ Always wash your hands each time you handle a new ingredient.

★ Don't ever use metal in the microwave.

★ Check to make sure all appliances are unplugged when you leave the kitchen.

Cook ... ITALIAN

E-Z PARTY PIZZAS

You Need (for 4-6 guests):

★ Package of 6 English muffins

★ 1 can tomato sauce

★ 1 package shredded mozzarella cheese

★ 1 stick pepperoni, mushrooms, or whatever topping you want

★ Dried oregano

What to Do:

1. Halve muffins and toast them.
2. Place muffins on a small baking sheet and spread each half with tomato sauce.
3. Sprinkle cheese over top and season with oregano.
4. Thinly slice pepperoni, mushrooms, or whatever topping you prefer and place evenly over cheese.
5. Place in oven or toaster oven. Broil for 2–3 minutes, or until cheese melts.

THE ORIGIN OF PIZZA DATES BACK TO A REAL-LIFE PRINCESS! IT WAS CREATED IN NAPLES, ITALY, ESPECIALLY FOR PRINCESS MARGHERITA. THE RED (TOMATO), GREEN (BASIL), AND WHITE (CHEESE) STAND FOR THE COLORS OF THE ITALIAN FLAG.

Jessie Knows!

CHEESY MEXICAN PIZZAS

You Need (for 4-6 guests):

★ 1 package soft taco-size flour tortillas

★ 1 can refried beans

★ 1 package shredded cheddar and/or Monterey Jack cheese

What to Do:

1. Spread a spoonful of refried beans on each tortilla.

2. Sprinkle shredded cheese over the beans.

3. Place under the broiler or in a toaster oven until cheese is bubbly.

4. Cut into wedges with a pizza cutter.

5. Serve with chips, salsa, and guacamole.

Jessie Knows!

WHEN IN DOUBT ABOUT WHAT FOOD TO SERVE, SCAN A COOKBOOK OR TAKE-OUT MENUS FOR GOOD IDEAS. DON'T FORGET TO PLAY MUSIC THAT GOES ALONG WITH YOUR THEME.

Cook . . . *Luau*

You Need (for 4-6 guests):

★ Large bowl and paper cups

★ 1 cup cold cranberry juice

★ 1 cup cold orange juice

★ 1 cup cold apple juice

★ 1 cup cold pineapple juice

★ 3 cups cold ginger ale or lemon-lime soda

★ Ice

★ Frozen pineapple chunks

What to Do:

★ Mix cold juices together in a large punch bowl.

★ Add ice, frozen pineapple, and soda just before serving.

Serve with:

• CHICKEN FINGERS

• STICKY WHITE RICE

• TROPICAL FRUIT SALAD INCLUDING PINEAPPLE, APPLES, GRAPES, BANANAS, TINY MARSHMALLOWS, AND SHREDDED COCONUT

Jessie Knows!

HAUOLI IS THE HAWAIIAN WORD FOR "HAPPY," AND THIS PUNCH WILL MAKE YOUR PARTY A HAPPY ONE!

Other Fun Food Ideas:

★ Order take-out cold sesame noodles and slice fresh cucumber on top. Don't forget to ask for chopsticks for everyone! Did you know the name chopstick is a variation on the Chinese word kuai-za, meaning "quick ones"?

★ Instead of a big meal, have a tea party! Serve finger sandwiches with thinly sliced turkey, cheese, and honey mustard on white bread. Don't forget to cut off the crusts and cut the sandwiches into triangles.

★ Who can forget about the sweet stuff? Dessert ideas that always work well:

• Make your own ice-cream sundaes.
• Bake cookies together and eat 'em while the chocolate is still melted.
• Make cupcakes baked in ice-cream cones (check online for recipes).

Movie-Marathon Party

Make your movie party a BLOCKBUSTER!

★ Design movie party invitations to look like actual movie tickets.

★ Rent at least two or three movies. Mix it up: spooky, romantic, and even cartoons.

★ While watching a movie with friends, don't be afraid to talk back to the screen. Sometimes when the dialogue is moving slowly, your own goofy lines will be the ones to crack everyone up.

★ See how many movie bloopers you can spot. The first person who finds three gets a prize.

★ Do a costume and setting critique. What would you have done to make the movie better?

POP TO IT!

Instead of popping plain corn, why not try some interesting flavors? While the popcorn is still hot, sprinkle on:

★ Butter (either melted or powdered)
★ Powdered ranch dressing packet
★ Cinnamon and sugar mix
★ Parmesan cheese
★ Peanuts, raisins, and mini chocolate-chips

Four-Star Friendship!

Whenever we get together to watch a movie, we imagine that we're the stars . . . .

Sometimes we play best friends. . . .

Sometimes we fight over who gets to be the villain. . . .

And we always take home the Academy Award!

Spa-tacular Fun!

School is hard work! So, why not invite your friends over for a little pampering? Creating an instant spa at home isn't so hard. All you need:

★ Everyone wearing loose clothes (staying comfy is key)

★ Pitcher of cold water with cut-up lemons
  (just like they serve in a real spa)

★ Homemade lavender sachets (to smell good)

★ Mellow mood music (instrumental is best)

YOU GLOW, GIRL!

Face Up to It

CITRUS MASK

Mix 1 teaspoon of **PLAIN YOGURT** and the juice of 1/4 of an **ORANGE** (squeezed into a cup). Then dip your fingers into the mixture and smooth onto your face. This mask's bonus: Orange has vitamin C, which is good for your skin.

SUGAR MASK

Mix a **RAW SUGAR PACKET** with a few drops of **OLIVE OR ALMOND OIL** (increase amounts of each depending on how much you need). Rub onto your face gently without getting into your eyes. Rinse off. Great for exfoliating.

APPLE MASK

Grate one **APPLE** and mix with 2 tablespoons of **HONEY** to make a mask. Smooth over skin and let sit for 10 minutes, then rinse off. Great for oily skin.

OATMEAL MASK

Add just enough warm water to a handful of loose plain **OATMEAL** to form a paste and then massage into your skin. Rinse off. Great for all skin types.

29

What Is Aromatherapy?

It's one of the oldest—5,000 years to be exact—methods of healing. Ancient cultures used it. Egyptians used to extract the oils from aromatic (aka scented) plants. Chinese civilizations wrote herbal books to show plants and their uses. East Indians used dried and fresh herbs for scented massage to make people feel better.

The word exfoliate means to remove dead skin cells. You rub gently to get the circulation going in your face and other skin areas. But Libby always tells me to be sure to rinse off the mask with cool water.

Jessie Knows!

Absolutely! Taking good care of your skin is important if you want to look good! But don't forget—if you have any allergies or sensitive skin, be careful about what you apply to your face. Test a small patch of your skin with lotions or masks first, and then try them on your face.

Best Friend Manicure Marathon

What better way to bond than by doing each other's nails? Fun!

Paint Your Nails 101

1 Clean your hands, especially around the nail bed.

2 Apply a clear base coat to the nail. Using this is important because it protects the nail from staining if you use dark polish. Plus, it smooths out little ridges in your nail.

3 Once the base coat is dry, apply the first coat of color polish. Remember to leave a slight gap between the nail and the cuticle.

4 Apply a second coat of polish after the first coat dries.

5 Finally, apply a clear topcoat. It gives a nice shine to the nail and protects the nail color. Use the topcoat to seal the end of the nail. A few days later, you can reapply more topcoat so the nail color lasts longer.

There are some easy designs you can paint on fingernails and toenails by using different colors of polish. Wait until the base coat is dry before painting the images. And apply the topcoat last.

Peace sign

Snowman

Smiley face

Lightning bolts

Star and moon

Flower

A•B•C Letters

TOE-riffic!

Don't forget your feet. Having friends on hand makes giving pedicures a snap. You can take turns painting one another's toenails. But before you paint, get your feet relaxed and softened.

FOOT SOAK

Mix together ¼ cup liquid soap with ¼ cup honey and ½ cup almond oil. Pour some into a hot bathtub and let it bubble up. Then have everyone sit on the tub edge and soak. Honey is great because it traps and seals in moisture, leaving the skin on your feet supersoft.

FOOT REST

Massage feet with your favorite lotion. Then wrap feet in plain plastic bags. Seal the edges with a rubber band for at least 15 minutes while your feet completely absorb the lotion. Now, that's soft!

DIVA Hair Dos and Don'ts

Get your friends together for a major hair makeover session. Have everyone put on a colorful feather boa for primping and take turns creating your hair masterpieces. All you need is a lot of imagination!

You Need:

Bobby pins

Combs and brushes

Lots of mousse and hair spray

Little paper umbrellas

Barrettes

Little elastic hair bands

Pipe cleaners

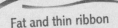

Fat and thin ribbon

Hair Hints

★ Make groovy-looking zigzag middle or side parts.

★ Pull back sections of hair with small elastic bands or ribbons.

★ Create fabulously messy or sensationally slick updos using different bobby pins and barrettes.

★ Have a braid-athon to see who makes the most interesting 'do—weaving in the pipe cleaners or ribbons as you go.

MORE Makeover Madness

Play This!

Get your friends to bring makeup—from blushers and eyeliner to lipstick and powder. Then pair off. One person in each pair will get a makeover. The only catch: The person applying the makeup is blindfolded! Don't forget to take before and after photographs.

Host Your Own Fashion Shoot!

Who says America's top models get to have all the fun? Turn your bedroom or basement hallway into a runway. Dim the lights, turn up the music, and have your friends strut their stuff.

Who's YOUR Style Sister?

I'm an artsy girl. To make over in my style, try wearing vintage clothes and bright colors.

I'M A GIRLY GIRL. TO MAKE OVER IN MY STYLE, GO FOR LACY AND SOFT FABRICS.

I'm a glam girl. To make over in my style, wear things that sparkle—a lot.

I'm a casual girl. To make over in my style, put on your sweatpants and just chill.

FINDING YOUR STYLE
by Sam

The key to your own style is simple—
YOU! Ask yourself: What's comfortable?
What's easy? What clothes, shoes, and
accessories make you feel the most like
you?

Here's what I do:

- Shop in different stores to find what I like best.

- Raid Mom's closet (or my BFF's closet) to try new things.

- Flip through magazines.

- Pick someone I admire and emulate her style.

- Dress down for comfort.

- Dress up for fun . . . but NOT to impress anyone!

The Art of Being Friends

Art, Talent, and Music Keep Friends Bonded 4-Ever!

- Every friendship needs a lot of art.

- Write funny notes to one another with cool borders and doodles.

- Tape pictures of one another onto your lockers.

- Draw some of the pictures yourself.

- Believe in magic—and in one another.

- Giggle together.

- Make a giant mural together.

- Celebrate one another no matter what.

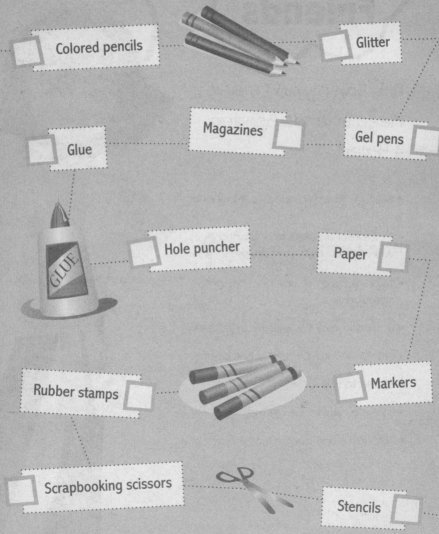

MUST-HAVE TOOLS and STUFF
for all of your art projects

Colored pencils

Glitter

Magazines

Gel pens

Glue

Hole puncher

Paper

Rubber stamps

Markers

Scrapbooking scissors

Stencils

Decorate Yourself!
Make Fashion Flip-flops

You Need:
- ★ A cheap pair of flip-flops (jelly or plastic only)
- ★ Small crystals, sequins, beads, silk flowers, or other decorative items
- ★ Heavy-duty glue (must dry clear)
- ★ Long tweezers

What to Do:

1 Decide on a design. Without gluing anything down (yet), arrange items where you want them to be.

2 Now apply a thick line of glue along the thong part of your flip-flop.

3 While the glue is wet, use the tweezers to grab your first item.

4 Place the item where you want to start the design, and continue adding pieces until you have both flip-flops done.

5 Leave the shoes to sit overnight to make sure the glue dries and your design is secure.

Make a Statement T-shirt!

I love squirrels!

Have a 🖤 for ART

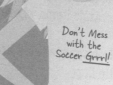

Don't Mess with the Soccer Grrrl!

You Need:

- ★ Plain white T-shirt
- ★ Fabric paint or markers

What to Do:

1. Think about something IMPORTANT you want to express.

2. Draw it. Write it. Put it on your T-shirt.

3. Let paint or markers dry. You may want to hand-wash your shirt before you wear it.

Collage-O-Rama

PIECES OF ME Collage

Snip out magazine photos of things you love, including cool words. Photocopy favorite pics of you and pals and lay everything out on a page. Once you have a design you like, glue it down. Somewhere on the collage, write and include a little poem or saying that has special meaning to you. Then use a gel pen to outline and decorate the edges.

Best Friends!

SPORTS STOP Collage

Cut out amazing photos of athletes, sports icons, etc. Don't forget to include shots of you playing sports, too. Then add in sporty souvenirs like ticket stubs, a bowling score sheet, a golf tee card, or other stuff like that. Find stickers of basketballs, soccer balls, tennis rackets, or other sporty stuff and stick around the edges.

3-D GLAMOUR Collage

Make a collage that really pops! Keep a folder of your ultimate fashion shots taken from different magazines, catalogs, or your own camera. Then get a piece of foam core and cut it into the shape of some smaller images. Glue the foam shapes and magazine photos together—they will be the 3-D part of your collage. You can decorate all over with glitter glue, ribbon, and other details, too.

IN THE GARDEN Collage

Tear out (leaving rough edges) photos of trees and flowers from home and gardening magazines (maybe Mom has some on the coffee table?). Make a garden on the page. After everything has been arranged and pasted, wait a moment before gluing down real dried flowers on top. This makes a great collage for fall foliage as well as summer wildflowers.

Make a Living Collage

★ Get a bulletin board up in your room.

★ Purchase a small package of thumbtacks.

★ Tack up photos, souvenirs, postcards, newspaper clippings, and ripped-out magazine images you love.

★ Arrange everything—and then change it all the very next day. A living collage will change with your mood. Over time, see how the design evolves. Invite your friends to add their own pictures!

Make the Ultimate Friendship SCRAPBOOK

You Need:

★ Blank notebook

★ Crayons or markers

★ Scissors

★ Magazine clippings

★ Glue

What to Do:

1 Decorate a blank notebook with the letters of the alphabet.

2 Pick one attribute about a friend that starts with one letter of the alphabet. Create a page about that letter—and that person. So for the letter A, paste a picture of Rachel with an artist's smock. Her "A" word is Art. On the smock, glue pictures of her paintings, photos, etc. You can also glue words that begin with the letter, like "Amazing," "Artsy," or "Anything Goes."

3 If your notebook is spiral bound, weave a ribbon through the binding when you are finished. If, after going through the entire alphabet, there is still room left in the notebook, save it and make other scrapbook pages dedicated to special events like birthdays, music recitals, or anything having to do with your friendship.

Make a scrapbook page called KEEP THE BEAT! Glue bits of sheet music to the page, or rewrite the lyrics from a song that perfectly describes your friendship. Then put a photo of your best pals at the center.

Make a YUMMY YUMMY page for every party you have as a group! Don't forget to glue down party souvenirs, too, like programs, tickets, postcards, or anything else clever.

Plan a specific scrapbook photo shoot for your album. Get totally spiffed up and take PRETTY PORTRAITS. Then get film developed or print the photos off your computer, arrange them, and glue onto a page. Decorate with glitter, sequins, and anything flashy.

PUT A BOOKWORM PAGE IN YOUR SCRAPBOOK. THIS REQUIRES A LITTLE MORE CLEVER THINKING—BUT IT WILL LOOK SOOOOO COOL. DRAW AN OUTLINE OF A BOOK AND THEN TITLE IT WITH SOMETHING THAT SPEAKS TO YOUR FRIEND OR GROUP OF FRIENDS. INSIDE EACH BOOK OUTLINE, PASTE PHOTOS OR REWRITE A FRIEND'S FAMILIAR QUOTES.

When You Wish Upon a Star

Sometimes friendship bonding happens when you all make WISHES together. One rainy weekend, the four of us had a Fortune-telling Saturday at my house. Dad blew up balloons and we put fortunes inside each one (we had to pop 'em to read 'em). We found one another's horoscopes online. Then we pretended we were all psychic. (I think sometimes Rachel really is!)

Tokens of good luck

- ★ Four-leaf clover
- ★ Rabbit's foot
- ★ Unicorn

Tokens of bad luck

- ★ Number 13
- ★ Black cat
- ★ Broken mirror

Make Your Own Crystal Ball

You Need:

- ★ Round Fishbowl
- ★ Poly-fil (get at a fabric store)
- ★ Paint pens
- ★ Gold or silver glitter

What to Do:

1 Stuff the bowl with cotton poly-fil—it will make your crystal ball look murky. You can even toss some glitter into the poly-fil to give it an extra-sparkly look.

2 Turn the bowl upside down so the open part is down.

3 Paint squiggly lines and words and little moons and stars all over—covering as much of the glass as possible.

4 Dim the lights and use your imagination. . . . Who knows what secret messages may come to you or your friends!

What Does Your Handwriting Mean?

Ts crossed near top = You have high goals. *t*

Ts crossed with a swoosh = You are excited. *t*

Ts crossed down low = Are you feeling okay? *t*

Is dotted just above the I = You're a superperfectionist. *i*

Is dotted with a line and not a dot = You need a little elbow room. *i*

Loops and dips in letters = You're a very determined person. *hello*

Os open at the top = You're a very honest person. *Cool*

Lots of space between words or letters =
You are fearless/brave. *audition*

Squished words or letters = You don't like large groups. *SLEEPOVER*

Teeny letters = You have good concentration. *it's a secret*

Curly letters = You are super-emotional.   *best friends*

Wavy letters = You're spacing out.   *what did she say?*

Pressed-down-hard letters = You're an amazing friend.   *CALL ME!*

Words on upward slant = You like to laugh.   *giggle*

Straight up and down words = You can always be trusted.   *MISS YOU*

Slanted to the left = You're nervous.   *what's up?*

Slanted to the right = You will be hugely successful.   *see ya*

Libby

Jessie

Samantha

Rachel

What Do Dreams Mean?

BFF bonding happens in a BIG way when we look at our dreams together. Everyone has a different idea about how to interpret a dream. I usually look up symbols in a dream dictionary. These are some of the most common. But remember: Only you know what everything really means!

ANIMALS • To dream that you are fighting with an animal means that you are unhappy about some part of yourself.

BIRDS • Dreaming about birds means you have a cheery, positive outlook on life. If you see a bird's nest, you will probably get money.

FAIRY • When you see a fairy, it means you want to get advice on something. P.S. If you want advice—just turn to your friends!

FALLING • Falling through the sky without being afraid means you are going through a hard time—but you will do well. If you are afraid when you fall, it means that you are feeling out of control about something in your life. If you fall through water, it means that you are feeling ultra-emotional right now.

MOON • A full moon means that something has just ended. A new moon means that something is just beginning. A crescent moon means that something is changing.

SKY • A clear blue sky means happiness. A cloudy sky means sadness.

SKYSCRAPER • Anyone who sees a skyscraper in her dream has big ambitions and desires. You always aim high at whatever you do.

STARS • Stars symbolize fate and luck. If you see these in your dream, you have a strong wish to be famous.

WATER • Water is commonly known as a symbol of your mind. If you dream about boiling water, it means that you are angry about something. Calm, clear water in your dream signifies that you are peaceful. Muddy or dirty water means that you are feeling negative.

Dream Big

Here are TEN cool questions to ask your friends when you talk about dreams—or when you keep your own dream journal.

What am I doing in this dream?

What do I feel in this dream?

In the dream, who are the main characters?

Did I dream of actual people or imaginary people? Who are they?

Is anyone being hurt, chased, or saved?

What features or symbols stand out most in the dream?

What would I like to avoid in my dream?

Does the dream trigger any memories?

What is the dream's positive message for me?

What do my friends think of the dream?

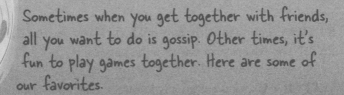

Boredom Busters

(Made Especially for Bonding)

Sometimes when you get together with friends, all you want to do is gossip. Other times, it's fun to play games together. Here are some of our favorites.

Truth or Dare

Everyone decides before a question is asked whether she wants to take "truth" or "dare." If you take "truth," it means you must answer the question honestly. If you take "dare," it means you must complete a task. If you cannot do the task, then you must answer the question.

Sample Questions:

★ If you could be anyone else in the whole world, who would it be?

★ If you could marry anyone, who would it be?

★ What is the craziest thing you've ever done?

★ What is the most embarrassing thing you've ever done?

Sample Dares:

★ Attempt to stand on your head.

★ Talk to a chair in a restaurant full of people and pretend it talks back to you.

★ Do the chicken dance in front of someone's parents.

★ Eat a packet of ketchup.

Sardines

This is like backward hide-and-seek. Only one player hides. The other players split up as seekers and try to find the hider. But instead of announcing when the hider is found, the seeker hides along with the hider. Soon almost all the seekers are actually hiding, packed into a hiding space like . . . you guessed it . . . SARDINES! The game lasts until the last seeker finds the group.

In the Manner of the Word

One player is sent out of the room while the others meet. The group then decides upon an adverb which the player will have to guess. Clues to this word will be acted out by the group. When the player returns to the room, she then asks the group to "do something in the manner of the word." So, for example, if the chosen adverb was "quickly," then the group will need to do something very fast. The player who left the room must continue to ask questions until she guesses the word.

Some adverbs that work well:

★ Angrily	★ Hotly	★ Sleepily
★ Charmingly	★ Jokingly	★ Timidly
★ Clumsily	★ Nastily	★ Tremblingly
★ Gently	★ Powerfully	★ Wisely
★ Heavily	★ Sadly	

MASH (aka Mansion/Apartment/Shack/House) •

You Need:
★ Blank pieces of paper (one for each friend) and pens

What to Do:
★ Make a grid on the page—divide into six columns. Title the columns as follows:

Boys | Colors | Cars | Kids | Cities | Occupations

★ Fill in five answers for each column.
Under "Boys," write down the name of five boys from your school.
Under "Colors," put down five of your favorites.
Under "Cars," put down the names of five different vehicles (you can write down Jeep, school bus, tractor—anything).
Under "Kids," write down five numbers, small or large.
Under "Cities," write down five places, near or far.
Under "Occupations," insert five names of jobs you find interesting (or bizarre!).

★ When you have finished filling in all the columns, have your friend choose a number from 1 to 10.

★ Counting down and up and down through the columns, cross off every item at the number your friend chose until you are left with one item in each column.

★ The game will then tell your future as follows: the boy you will marry, the color and type of car you will drive; the number of kids you will have; the city where you will live; and your job. Whose is the silliest?

JOIN THE CLUB!

Sometimes it seems like everyone belongs to a special club. But what about you and your friends? Hint: It's easy to belong to a club—if you make up your own!

Name the Club

Below are some suggested groups—but you can probably come up with better names! Use words that have special meaning to your group. Perhaps there is a nickname that works, or the name of the place where you all first met.

Elect Officers

Every club needs a roster of "officers" to help things run smoothly. You'll need a president, of course, to call order and set the agenda for each meeting. You might want to call your fearless leader something cooler, like "princess in charge." You'll also need a note-taker. Invent other necessary roles, like member-in-charge-of-snacking and official DJ.

Find a Place to Meet

Will you meet behind the library? In one of your bedrooms? In someone's tree house? Find a place that works for everyone, and meet there regularly.

Reading Club
Set Up Your Own Book Group

1. Choose a place and time where you will meet.

2. Choose books you want to read together. Reading for a group discussion is different from reading on your own. When you read for a group, you want to think about key ideas in the book, character motivations, writing style, and all the other things you can talk about together.

3. When you meet, have each member of your group come prepared with one question to ask about the book. Things you might ask:

   - How does the title relate to the book?
   - What character do you like best? Least?
   - What is the theme of the book?

SOMETIMES YOU CAN INVITE MOMS, DADS, AUNTS, OR GRANDMOTHERS TO JOIN YOUR READING GROUP. IT DOESN'T HAVE TO BE EXCLUSIVE TO JUST YOUR BEST FRIENDS.

Go Green Club

We _____(Your Names Here)_____ do swear to work together to find ways to help the environment. We will learn all we can about protecting nature and wildlife. We will volunteer our time to help. We will commit to helping make this world a greener, healthier, and better place.

What does it mean to be GREEN? So many things! If you're GREEN, you're considered "eco-friendly." You probably use natural products, are aware of wastefulness, use fuel and power efficiently, and you definitely care about global warming.

THE MOST IMPORTANT THING WE CAN DO IS RECYCLE. DID YOU KNOW THAT IF YOU THROW AWAY TWO ALUMINUM CANS, YOU WASTE MORE ENERGY THAN 1,000,000,000 (THAT'S ONE BILLION) OF THE WORLD'S POOREST PEOPLE USE A DAY? DID YOU ALSO KNOW THAT THE AVERAGE AMERICAN CREATES ABOUT 3.5 POUNDS OF TRASH A DAY? THAT'S SO DISGUSTING!

Top Ten Ways You Can Help the Environment
Right NOW, by Libby :>)

1 Turn off lights, TVs, stereos, and radios when not in use.

2 Use fans instead of air conditioners.

3 In winter, try wearing a sweater instead of turning up the heat.

4 Use less hot water.

5 Take public transportation, ride your bike, or walk.

6 Use recycled paper. Reuse old papers.

7 Plant trees, especially if you ever cut one down.

8 Buy products with little or no packaging.

9 If you have a good zoo nearby, support it, especially if they help breed endangered animals.

10 Cut up your plastic six-pack soda rings before throwing them out. They can strangle unsuspecting animals or birds that might get into trash dumps.

Lights, Camera, Action!

Making Your Own Play Production

Turn your favorite book or TV show episode into a play—or make up your own brilliant story. Decide who will write the script, who will get a starring role, who will be in charge of props, and other important details. Find a regular time to meet and practice. When you're ready to perform, set up a time to showcase your masterpiece for Mom, Dad, and whoever else wants to see.

Although I don't personally get stage jitters, I know a lot of people who do. But don't let that turn you off the idea of making a play! Pretending to be another character is so much fun. Who would you be if you could be any character in any story? I know I'd be Dorothy in The Wizard of Oz. Totally!

Dance-athon

Spin your favorite tunes and get exercise at the same time!

The next time you have your friends over, remember this: Nothing says bonding like aerobic exercise. Turn up the Top 40 tunes and get in shape together. Choose different music "themes" (country, pop, rock, rap) and have mini dance contests among yourselves. And if you work up a really big sweat, cool down with some of the awesome spa suggestions on pages 28–34.

Exercising with friends makes workout time pass so much faster. Sometimes the four of us will plan to go for a jog around the reservoir or we'll put in one of my mom's yoga DVDs and pretend we're in this exclusive yoga class, like the kind movie stars take. Libby loves that!

Passing Notes

Passing notes is one of the BEST ways to stay connected with my BFs. We do it in school between classes or during lunch. I sometimes stick notes in my friends' backpacks so they find them later. And whenever anyone goes away on a trip, we always write "plane letters." These are long friendship notes that can be read whenever you feel homesick!

TRY THIS!

Fan Mail

No, this isn't a letter to a movie star—it's for your good buddy. To make genuine fan mail, you turn your note into an actual fan. Take a piece of paper and fold it accordion-style. Then take a marker and, squishing the fan together, write a secret message on the side of the folds. Open up the fan. It will appear as if you've written a note made up of dots, but when your friend folds the fan, she will be able to read the message.

Cut-up Notes

Write a note starting each thought/sentence on a new line. Then cut the lines apart. When you're done, you should have a pile of paper strips. Put these into an envelope with instructions on how to put the pieces of the puzzle back together. It won't prevent all snooping   but it will prevent anyone from quickly glancing at your entire note. Don't forget to tell your friend how to read it!

ONE OF THE WAYS I LIKE TO KEEP MY NOTES HUSH—HUSH IS TO WRITE THEM IN CODE.

I never sign a single note without writing some kind of goofy rhyme. I like it when my notes get a laugh! Like, "Roses are red, violets are blue, I missed you at recess, so phooey on you!" My grandmother told me this one: "Tell me quick before I faint. Is we friends or is we ain't?" My friends usually like to see what I'll make up next.

I always doodle all over my notes. They look so cool!

61

Log Online Club

If you're not passing handwritten notes, you're probably passing notes online via e-mail or instant messaging. There are important things to know about being online friends, too.

Six Stay-Safe Cyber Rules

BY JESSIE

1. LET YOUR PARENTS KNOW IMMEDIATELY IF YOU FIND SOMETHING SCARY OR THREATENING ON THE INTERNET.

2. NEVER GIVE OUT YOUR NAME, ADDRESS, TELEPHONE NUMBER, PASSWORD, SCHOOL NAME, PARENTS' NAMES, OR ANY OTHER PERSONAL INFORMATION.

3. NEVER AGREE TO MEET FACE-TO-FACE WITH SOMEONE YOU MEET ONLINE.

4. NEVER RESPOND TO MESSAGES THAT HAVE BAD WORDS OR SEEM SCARY OR JUST WEIRD.

5. NEVER ENTER AN AREA THAT CHARGES FOR SERVICES WITHOUT ASKING YOUR PARENTS FIRST.

6. NEVER SEND A PICTURE OF YOURSELF TO ANYONE WITHOUT YOUR PARENTS' PERMISSION.

Don't Forget! Being Online Has Its Own "Chattiquette"

1 Don't send chain letters. Some sites will terminate your membership if they know you send them.

2 Don't send angry messages, even if someone tries to get you into an argument.

3 Use upper- and lowercase letters. ALL UPPERCASE LETTERS TELL A READER THAT YOU ARE SHOUTING. That's not nice.

Your IM Chat-a-log

U2
You too

JK
Just kidding

L8R
Later

LOL
Laugh out loud, or lots of love

CYA
See ya!

TMI
Too much information

PPL
People

BTW
By the way

NEVER 4-GET!
ALWAYS REMEMBER!

Best buds always let you be yourself — even if you look a little bit different...

Groovy friends don't get bummed... they go shopping!

YOUR FRIENDS KNOW HOW TO READ BETWEEN THE LINES — TO SEE THE TRUE YOU.

No matter how fast I run, good friends always know how to keep up with me.

Remember that when it comes to friendship, being bonded is what counts most. Try new things together. Share your friends' favorite games, sports, activities, and fashion tips. Here's the real deal: When you believe in each other, everything else makes sense. And best friendships really *can* last forever.